PREVENTING JOB BURNOUT

Beverly A. Potter, Ph.D.

Illustrations by **Mary Swetnika**

CRISP PUBLICATIONS, INC.
Los Altos, California

PREVENTING JOB BURNOUT

CREDITS

Editor: **Michael Crisp**
Production: **Consulting Psychologists Press**
Cover Design: **Carol Harris**
Artwork: **Mary Swetnika**

Copyright © 1987 by Beverly A. Potter
Printed in the United States of America

Crisp books are distributed in Canada by Reid Publishing, Ltd., P.O. Box 7267, Oakville, Ontario, Canada L6J 6L6.

In Australia by Career Builders, P.O. Box 1051 Springwood, Brisbane, Queensland, Australia 4127.

And in New Zealand by Career Builders, P.O. Box 571, Manurewa, New Zealand.

Library of Congress Catalog Card Number 86-72077
Potter, Beverly, A.
Preventing Job Burnout
ISBN 0-931961-23-8

PREFACE

If you've ever had a bad day at work (and who hasn't?), then you have an inkling of how immobilizing burnout can be. If having bad days at work has become the standard rather than the exception, then it is likely that you are a victim of job burnout. But work doesn't have to be a chore. There are specific actions you can take, starting today, to beat job burnout and transform work pressure into productivity. Introducing you to these techniques and showing you how to use them is the purpose of this book.

PREVENTING JOB BURNOUT is a practical guide. You will learn what job burnout is, what causes it, and how to assess the burnout potential of your job. And you will learn how to identify what is eroding your motivation and enthusiasm for your job. More importantly, you will learn eight strategies for beating job burnout and preventing it in the future.

PREVENTING JOB BURNOUT is a fun book. As you complete the exercises and carry out the suggested activities you will learn more about yourself, particularly how you function—on and off—the job. Learning about yourself can be fun, and knowing yourself better increases your ability to control your job and your life. When you feel you can control what happens to you, your health tends to improve, your relationships tend to get better, and you tend to perform better.

PREVENTING JOB BURNOUT is not a book to be read one time from cover to cover. It is a book to return to again and again for refueling and new ideas about how to handle difficult situations on the job. Enjoy.

Beverly A. Potter

ABOUT THIS BOOK

PREVENTING JOB BURNOUT is not like most books. It has a unique "self-paced" format that encourages a reader to become personally involved. Designed to be "read with a pencil," there are exercises, activities, assessments and cases that invite participation.

PREVENTING JOB BURNOUT can be used effectively in a number of ways. Here are some possibilities:

— Individual Study. Because the book is self-instructional, all that is needed is a quiet place, some time and a pencil. Completing the activities and exercises should provide not only valuable feedback, but also practical ideas for self-improvement.

— Workshops and Seminars. This book is ideal for pre-assigned reading prior to a workshop or seminar. With the basics in hand, more time can be spent on concept extensions and applications. The book is also effective when distributed at the beginning of a session.

— Remote Location Training. Copies can be sent to those not able to attend "home office" training sessions.

— Informal Study Groups. Thanks to the format, brevity and low cost, this book is ideal for "brown-bag" or other informal group sessions.

There are other possibilities that depend on the objectives of the user. One thing for sure, even after it has been read, this book will serve as excellent reference material which can be easily reviewed. Good luck!

CONTENTS

Preface   i

About This Book   ii

What Is Job Burnout?   2

Motivational Nutrients   6

Revitalizing Motivation Through Personal Power   18

❖ Self-Management:
    First Path to Personal Power   20

❖ Stress Management:
    Second Path to Personal Power   32

❖ Building Social Support:
    Third Path to Personal Power   44

❖ Skill Building:
    Fourth Path to Personal Power   48

❖ Tailoring The Job:
    Fifth Path to Personal Power   52

❖ Changing Jobs:
    Sixth Path to Personal Power   60

❖ Think Powerfully:
    Seventh Path to Personal Power   64

❖ Detached Concern:
    Eighth Path to Personal Power   70

Review   74

About the Author   76

> **Without work, all life goes rotten, but when work is soulless, life stifles and dies.**
>
> **—Albert Camus**

WHAT IS JOB BURNOUT?

Job burnout, an impairment of motivation to work, is increasingly common in today's complex world. It begins with small warning signals: feelings of frustration, emotional outbursts, withdrawal, health problems, alienation, substandard performance and the increased use of drugs and alcohol.

If unheeded, these symptoms can progress until a person dreads going to work. Even worse, burnout tends to spread to all aspects of a person's life. Rarely is a person burned out at work, yet energized and enthusiastic at home.

BURNOUT SYMPTOMS

Burnout Symptoms

Following are the common symptoms of job burnout:

Negative emotions: Occasional feelings of frustration, anger, depression, dissatisfaction and anxiety are normal parts of living and working. But people caught in the burnout cycle usually experience these negative emotions more and more often until they become chronic. Eventually, the person complains of emotional fatigue.

Interpersonal problems: Feeling emotionally drained makes interacting with people on the job and at home more difficult. When inevitable conflicts arise, the burnout victim is likely to overreact with an emotional outburst or intense hostility. This makes communication with co-workers, friends and family increasingly difficult. The victim also tends to withdraw from social interactions. The tendency to withdraw is most pronounced among helping professionals who often become aloof and inaccessible to the very people they are expected to help.

Health problems: As the person's emotional reserves are depleted and the quality of relationships deteriorates, the burnout victim's physical resilience declines. Minor ailments, such as colds, headaches, insomnia and backaches become more frequent. There is a general feeling of being tired and rundown.

Declining performance: During the burnout process a person may become bored and unable to get excited about projects. In other cases, the burnout victim may discover that concentrating on projects is increasingly difficult. Efficiency suffers and quality of output declines.

Substance abuse: To cope with the stress associated with job conflict and declining performance, the person will often consume more alcohol, eat more or eat less, use more drugs, smoke more cigarettes, and drink more coffee. This increased substance abuse further compounds problems.

Feelings of meaninglessness: Feelings of "so what" and "why bother" become more and more predominant. This is particularly common among burnout victims who were once very enthusiastic and dedicated. Enthusiasm is replaced by cynicism. Working seems pointless.

BURNOUT VICTIMS

Helping professionals, such as social workers, nurses, teachers and police officers, are the hardest hit by burnout. Often they become cynical and negative, and sometimes overtly hostile toward their clients. Other burnout-prone professions include: those that require exacting attention, such as air traffic controllers; those that deal with life or death decisions, such as heart surgeons; those that require working under demanding time schedules such as television news crews; or those that involve detailed work, such as book-keeping; that are socially criticized, such as nuclear plant supervisors; and many others. The fact is, *any* person, in any profession, at any level can become a candidate for burnout. No one is immune.

ARE YOU BURNING OUT?

NO ONE IS IMMUNE!

Are You Burning Out?

Review your life over the last six months, both at work and away from work. Then read each of the following items and rate how often the symptom is true of you.

1 = rarely	3 = often true	5 = usually true
2 = sometimes true	4 = frequently true	

____ 1. I feel tired even when I've gotten adequate sleep.

____ 2. I often feel dissatisfied.

____ 3. I feel sad for no apparent reason.

____ 4. I am forgetful.

____ 5. I am irritable and snap at people.

____ 6. I am withdrawn.

____ 7. I have trouble sleeping.

____ 8. I get sick a lot.

____ 9. My attitude about work is "why bother."

____ 10. I get into conflicts with others.

____ 11. My job performance is not up to par.

____ 12. I use alcohol and/or drugs to feel better.

____ 13. Communicating with others is a strain.

____ 14. I can't concentrate like I once could.

____ 15. I am easily bored.

____ 16. I work hard but accomplish little.

____ 17. I feel frustrated.

____ 18. I don't like going to work.

____ 19. Social activities are draining.

____ 20. Sex is not worth the effort.

Scoring:

20–40 You're doing well.
41–60 You're okay if you take preventative action.
61–80 You're a candidate for burnout.
81–100 You're burning out.

MOTIVATIONAL NUTRIENTS

Just as the body needs vitamins and proteins, certain "nutrients" are also essential to sustain high motivation. These include getting "wins" for good work and having feelings of control.

Burnout is neither a physical ailment nor a neurosis, even though it has both physical and psychological effects. It is an inability to mobilize enough interest to act. Motivation to perform is diminished or extinguished. To prevent job burnout, you need to maintain motivation.

"Wins" for good work

Motivation is determined largely by what happens *after* you act. You simply do not continue to do things that make you lose or that bring you nothing. If your motivation is to remain high, you must get "wins" for performing.

POSITIVE WINS

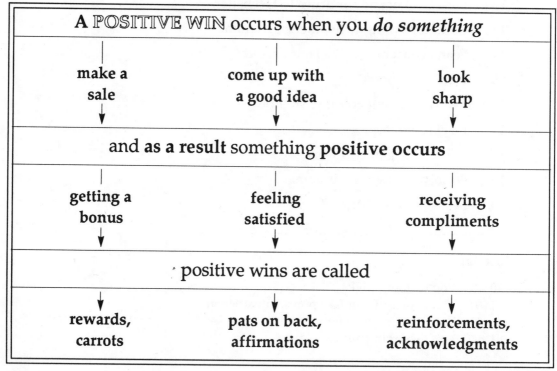

A POSITIVE WIN occurs when you *do something*		
make a sale	come up with a good idea	look sharp
and as a result something **positive occurs**		
getting a bonus	feeling satisfied	receiving compliments
positive wins are called		
rewards, carrots	pats on back, affirmations	reinforcements, acknowledgments

> *An old joke*
>
> **First Man, while banging his head:**
> "Oh, this really hurts!"
>
> **Second Man:** "Well, why are you doing it?"
>
> **First Man:** "Because it feels so good when I stop!"

NEGATIVE WINS

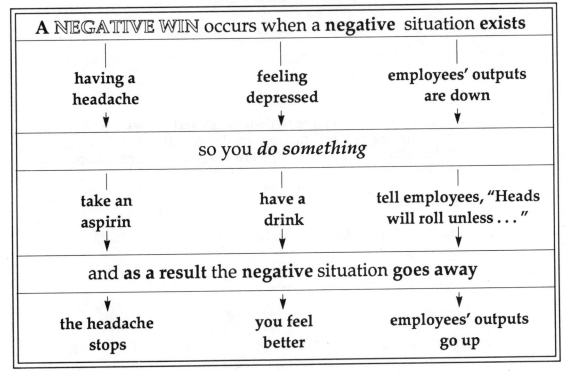

A NEGATIVE WIN occurs when a **negative** situation **exists**		
having a headache	feeling depressed	employees' outputs are down
so you *do something*		
take an aspirin	have a drink	tell employees, "Heads will roll unless . . ."
and **as a result** the **negative** situation **goes away**		
the headache stops	you feel better	employees' outputs go up

IDENTIFY THE WINS

What positive and negative wins can you find in each of the following cases? What do you predict will happen in the future?

Case 1: Sally worked all weekend putting the final touches on her presentation to the sales force. When she made the presentation, she had to pause several times for the laughter at her jokes to subside. When she finished, the sales reps gave her an enthusiastic standing ovation.

Sally's wins _____

In the future Sally will probably _____

_____

_____

Case 2: Bill's boss hates idleness. If she thinks Bill doesn't have enough to do she quickly assigns him more work. Bill just noticed his boss patrolling the aisles so he quickly lowered his head and wrote meaningless notes on a pad. Bill's boss smiled as she walked by his desk.

Bill's wins _____

In the future Bill will probably _____

_____

_____

Case 3: Supervisor Ralph has an open door policy and Jim takes advantage of it. Three or four times a day, Jim drops by Ralph's office to tell him the latest gossip from the sports page. Ralph always stops what he's doing and listens carefully.

Jim's wins _____

In the future Jim will probably _____

_____

_____

See page 10 for a discussion of the cases.

Case 4: Ralph was recently promoted to supervisor. To prepare for the job he took a training course where he learned about the importance of an open door policy. Ralph implemented it and people drop by several times a day, but they rarely talk about work. His employee, Jim, told him that he's a "great guy to work for." Because of the constant interruptions, Ralph can't get his work done and must take it home at night. His wife has begun complaining because they never go out any more.

Ralph's wins _____

In the future Ralph will probably _____

_____

_____

Case 5: Even though Helen has taken several time management courses, she can't seem to break the procrastination habit. It was her responsibility to write a proposal for a million dollar grant. The fate of her department hung in the balance. As usual, Helen procrastinated. For two weeks she was paralyzed with guilt and fear. However, she finally got started and, with the help of some pills a friend gave her, managed to work straight through two nights with only a couple of 15-minute naps. She miraculously got the proposal done just in time. Feeling enormously relieved, Helen went home and collapsed.

Helen's wins _____

In the future Helen will probably _____

_____

_____

Case 6: Willie's boss, Hank, is easily rattled. Willie delights in getting Hank to react and baits him at every opportunity. Hank is particularly irritated when Willie is late. He's talked to Willie a number of times about it but Willie continues his lateness. Willie returned 15 minutes late from a break today and Hank was furious. Trying to be calm, Hank blurted out, "You're late again!" The gum Hank was chewing flew out of his mouth and hit Willie on the cheek. Knowing that several of the other guys were watching, Willie retorted, "I'm going to have you arrested for assault with a deadly weapon." Everyone in the office broke into uncontrollable laughter as Hank stomped off.

Willie's wins _____

In the future Willie will probably _____

_____

_____

Discussion

Case 1: Sally received two strong positive wins: the laughter and the standing ovation. Chances are she will continue putting extra time into her presentations and will tell a lot of jokes during the delivery.

Case 2: By looking busy, Bill gets the negative win of avoiding additional work. Bill will probably engage in meaningless activity in order to look busy whenever he sees his boss approaching his desk.

Case 3: Ralph's attention to Jim's talking about sports is a positive win for Jim. It's no wonder he drops into Ralph's office several times a day. As long as Ralph continues to listen to Jim's stories he should expect Jim to talk about sports.

Case 4: People dropping into Ralph's office and Jim's friendly comment are positive wins for Ralph. However, he's also receiving strong punishments. He cannot complete his work during the day; he has to work on it at home and his wife is complaining about it. Ralph is a good candidate for job burnout.

Case 5: Helen's procrastination habit is supported by negative wins. Her procrastination creates tremendous anxiety. When she finally does write the proposal and succeeds in avoiding disaster, she experiences relief, which feels very, very good. The cycle is compounded by her drug use. Helen is a good candidate for job burnout.

Case 6: Willie's lateness is supported by strong positive wins. Not only did he succeed in unnerving Hank and making him look foolish in front of everyone, he also received much admiration from the other guys. Willie will most likely continue being late.

Positive Win

Giving yourself pats on the back or self-acknowledgement is essential in developing "working for" motivation.

No Win Situations

Damned-if-you-do, damned-if-you-don't situations create feelings of helplessness which diminish motivation.

In Greek mythology, Susyphus, an evil king, was condemned to Hades to forever roll a big rock up the mountain which always rolled back down again. This version of Hell is suffered every day by people with forever full in-baskets, or who work under unrelenting pressure, or work with clients who don't get better.

Sustaining Motivation

To sustain motivation, you must see a cause and effect relationship between what you do and what happens to you. In other words, you must *feel* you can influence what happens to you, either good or bad, by what you *do*.

FEELINGS OF CONTROL ⟹

Motivation

POSITIVE	NEGATIVE

WORKING FOR

Positive Win:
Gaining a Positive

Praise
Satisfaction
Self-Respect
Raise/Promotion
Status/Fame
Challenge
Fun

{ such as **}**

WORK ENTHUSIAST

WORKING TO AVOID

Negative Win:
Avoiding a Negative

Debt
Job Loss
Criticism
Bad Marriage
Loneliness
Guilt

WORKAHOLIC

LEARNED HELPLESSNESS

Learned Helplessness: A Scientific Study

Two matched dogs were placed one at a time in a room with a shock grid floor. One *could do something* to turn off the shock, the other *could do nothing*.

When first shocked both dogs jumped, yelped and tried to figure out how to turn off the shock. The dog in the "controllable" situation had little difficulty learning to turn off the shock with a lever. Every time the dog was put in the room, it quickly turned off the shock. This dog was highly motivated.

In the "uncontrollable" situation there was nothing the second dog could do to turn off the shock. Just like the first dog, it tried to figure out how to turn off the shock until the dog learned it was helpless. Then the dog gave up and lay down on the floor and took the shock. This dog was no longer motivated to even try to escape.

Later, the dog that had learned it was helpless was put into the room with the lever for turning off the shock. But the dog just lay on the floor and took the shock. Even when the door was left wide open, the dog did not attempt to escape. It just lay there. The dog had learned that it was helpless and continued to act accordingly, even though the situation had changed.

When the dog "learned" it was helpless

- It stopped trying. Its <u>motivation</u> to escape <u>was extinguished</u>.
- The dog <u>exhibited</u> a lot of <u>negative emotions</u>. It yelped and growled, then it whimpered and eventually just lay there.
- Something happened that <u>interfered with</u> the dog's <u>ability to learn</u> that things had changed and it could do something.

Powerlessness at work can affect you in the same way

➤ Impaired motivation
➤ Negative emotions
➤ Inability to learn or adapt to changes

Feelings of powerlessness cause burnout.

DEMOTIVATING

Demotivating work situations similar to those shown below are key contributors to job burnout. Check those which may apply to your situation.

❑ **THE CRITICAL BOSS** — No matter how hard you try or how well you do, this boss always finds a nit to pick. Eventually, you feel helpless to satisfy this boss.

❑ **THE INCURABLE CLIENT** — Many helping professionals, such as social workers, have large caseloads of clients with nearly impossible problems. No matter how hard they try, how much they give, or how much they care the drug addicts continue to use drugs; the welfare recipients can't get work; and the delinquents end up back in juvenile hall.

❑ **LACK OF RECOGNITION** — Having one's work acknowledged is important, but good work often goes unnoticed. Civil service jobs, where promotions are based on seniority and not performance, are a good example. Other examples include housewives, secretaries, and clerks. Other forms of lack of recognition include:

> **Inadequate Pay:** When you work hard but feel underpaid, you can feel your efforts and outputs are not being adequately recognized.

> **Under-Employment:** If you have high aspirations and spent years in college preparing for work but are employed below your appropriate level, you can equate this with a lack of recognition. Baby boomers who must compete with millions of others to squeeze into a narrowing pyramid are particularly prone to this dilemma.

❑ **AMBIGUITY** — If you don't know what's expected, it is difficult to feel confident that you are doing the right thing in the right way. Chaotic and ambiguous work situations are common in rapidly expanding high tech firms. Examples of ambiguity are:

> **Lack of Information:** Ambiguity can manifest itself in a lack of enough information to complete your job. As a result you may be working hard on the wrong thing.

> **Lack of Clear Goals:** Jobs in rapidly expanding organizations, entrepreneurial operations, and poorly managed departments often suffer from lack of clear goals. Without clear goals, you have no target to aim at.

WORK SITUATIONS

❑ **TASKS WITHOUT END** — This is the in-basket that is always full, no matter how long or hard you work. This is the unending line of customers who eventually become faceless. This is assembly line work. This is any job that has no natural beginning and ending point.

❑ **NO WIN SITUATIONS** — There are jobs in which no matter what you do someone is dissatisfied. Some examples are:

> **Incompatible Demands:** If you work in matrix organizations where you report to two bosses you can be confronted with incompatible demands. One boss may want speed while the other wants quality. Producing both may not be possible. Jobs that require working across departmental boundaries are also plagued by incompatible demands. Marketing wants one thing while manufacturing wants another. Anyone interfacing between unions and management struggles with this problem.

> **Conflicting Roles:** This can be a woman executive who is expected to be supermom, superwife and star employee or a manager whose company expects her to travel and whose family want her at home.

> **Value Conflicts:** If you work in a sensitive field such as police work, IRS investigation, military, weapons research or nuclear power, you may face value conflicts. You believe in what you are doing and you strive to do a good job, yet everywhere you go people criticize you for the work you do.

❑ **WORK OVERLOAD** — A lot of work in and of itself is not demotivating as long as you feel you can control what happens and you receive adequate wins. You may be very tired, but motivation can remain high. An overload of work in the above categories, however, is a set-up for burnout.

What Is the Burnout Potential of Your Job?

Now that you have read and reacted to demotivating work situations, it is time to evaluate the burnout potential of your job. Answer the following questions as honestly as you can. How often do these situations bother you at work? Use the following rating scale:

(Rarely) 1 - 2 - 3 - 4 - 5 - 6 - 7 - 8 - 9 (Constantly)

Powerless

___ 1. I can't solve the problems assigned to me.
___ 2. I am trapped in my job with no options.
___ 3. I am unable to influence decisions that affect me.
___ 4. Priorities I must meet are constantly being changed.

No Information

___ 5. I am unclear about the responsibilities of my job.
___ 6. I am underqualified for the work I actually do.
___ 7. I don't have enough information to carry out my job.
___ 8. Others I work with are unclear about what I do.

Conflict

___ 9. I am caught in the middle.
___10. I am expected to satisfy conflicting demands.
___11. I disagree with co-workers.
___12. I disagree with my supervisor.
___13. I can't get what I need to carry out the job.

Overload

___14. My job interferes with my personal life.
___15. I have too much to do and too little time in which to do it.
___16. I must work on my own time.
___17. The size of my workload interferes with how well I do it.

Boredom

___18. I waste a lot of time in unproductive meetings.
___19. I have too little to do.
___20. I am overqualified for the work I actually do.
___21. My work is not challenging.
___22. The majority of my time is spent on routine tasks.

No Feedback

___23. I don't know what I am doing right and what I am doing wrong.
___24. I don't know what my supervisor thinks of my performance.

Punishment

___25. My supervisor is critical.
___26. Good work goes unnoticed.
___27. My work is unappreciated.
___28. I am not accepted by the people I work with.
___29. My progress on the job is not what it could be.
___30. Someone else got the promotion I deserved.

Alienation

___31. I am isolated from others.
___32. I lack confidence in management.
___33. The organization is insensitive to my individuality.
___34. I am "different" from the others and can't be myself at work.
___35. My work accomplishments are meaningless.

Cause and Effect

___36. I don't know the basis used to evaluate me.
___37. There is no relationship between my performance and my treatment.
___38. Popularity and politics are more important than performance.
___39. It doesn't matter how well or poorly I perform.
___40. I don't know what is expected of me.
___41. I don't know what I must do to get ahead.
___42. There is no relationship between how I perform and how I'm rated.

Value Conflict

___43. I must do things that are against my better judgement.
___44. I must make compromises in my values.
___45. My friends/family disapprove of what I do.

Scoring:

45–180   Low potential if you take preventative action.
181–270   Moderate potential. Develop a plan to correct problem areas.
271–450   High potential. Corrective action is vital.

REVITALIZING MOTIVATION THROUGH PERSONAL POWER

> The antidote for burnout is *personal power* or *a feeling of I-Can-Do.* That you can act to control your work.

Personal power can insulate you from the negative effects of many work situations. You feel in command by making a plan for action and using goals and objectives to carry out your plan. You become a winner because you refuel yourself with a sense of accomplishment and other "wins" independent of your boss or the organization.

Making the decision to take command and direct your life is the first and most difficult step to developing personal power. It is here that you may become ambivalent. Rebelling against control may be so much a part of you that when you attempt to take command of yourself, you blindly rebel. This can start a pattern of self-punishment, which reaffirms fears of being controlled.

Paths to Personal Power

There are eight paths to personal power, all of which will be discussed in detail through the remainder of this book. The paths that you can take to achieve personal power are:

❖ PATH 1: Self-Management

Effective self-management requires knowledge and skill. You probably acquired your self-managing skills informally, from parents and teachers. Consequently, you may not manage yourself effectively. Properly done, self-management increases your personal power because you can create situations in which you can give yourself the "wins" you need to sustain high motivation.

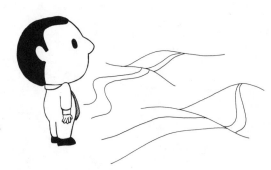

❖ PATH 2: Stress Management

It is important to know how your body and psyche function and which situations trigger your stress responses. This understanding can be used to raise and lower your tension level as needed. Personal power comes in knowing that, although you may not like the difficult situations, you *can* handle them. Such feelings enable you to rise to the occasion and to handle difficulties skillfully rather than avoid problem situations.

❖ PATH 3: Build a Support System

A strong social support system made up of family, friends and co-workers can help buffer you against the negative effects of stress. People with strong support systems tend to be healthier and live longer. It's vitally important that you take active measures to build and maintain your support system.

❖ PATH 4: Skill Building

Inevitably, you will encounter situations requiring skills you've not yet developed. Personal power comes from knowing how to arrange learning situations for yourself. When you know how to acquire the skills you need, you'll have confidence to tackle new challenges and handle the unexpected.

❖ PATH 5: Modify the Job

Almost every job has some leeway for tailoring it to better fit your workstyle. The ability to mesh a job to your style increases feelings of potency and enjoyment of work.

❖ PATH 6: Change Jobs

Sometimes the best solution is to change jobs. Too often, however, burnout victims will quit an unsatisfactory job without analyzing the source of dissatisfaction or exploring what is needed, and grab the next job that comes along. Sometimes the new job is as bad as, or even worse, than the old one. Personal power comes in knowing what you need in a job and knowing how to go out and find it.

❖ PATH 7: Mood Management with Thought Control

You may sometimes feel out of control in the face of your emotions. If so, you may be a victim of runaway thinking, and not knowing how to curb your thoughts, you respond to every red flag waved before you. Personal power comes in knowing how to empty your mind of negative chatter so that you can focus productivity on the moment and the tasks at hand.

❖ PATH 8: Detached Concern

Detached concern is a higher-order level of mental control in which personal power is gained by letting go. This is particularly important for those who work with people having serious or even impossible problems. It is the attachment to your notions of how things *ought to be* that can imprison you and make you feel helpless. As with the Chinese finger puzzle, it's only when you stop pulling that you can break loose.

SELF-MANAGEMENT

First Path to Personal Power

> The way you manage yourself has a direct impact on your motivation and job satsifaction. Good self-managers enjoy working because they get more done and give themselves more credit.
>
> If you use threats and criticism to make yourself work, procrastinate or demand perfection, you are probably far less productive than you could be. You can increase the quality of your work and perform excellently more often by improving your self-management abilities.

Managing yourself is not a matter of will power, rather it is an array of simple but effective techniques such as:

- ➤ Using fun to reward dull work
- ➤ Patting yourself on the back
- ➤ Indulging yourself contingently
- ➤ Breaking big jobs down into mangeable steps

The tools to help you improve self-management include:

- ➤ Setting goals
- ➤ Setting objectives

How to Set Goals

Personal Goal Setting

Goals are tools for helping you make decisions. Each day you encounter choices or forks in the road. When you have a goal, it is easier to make choices and to know which path to take. In other words, a goal acts as a beacon to point the way. Without goals, you can go around and around, never getting where you want to go. Once you achieve a goal, it is important to set another one. Following are some principles to keep in mind as you establish your personal goals:

1. Be Positive

State what you want to *do*. If you want to avoid or stop doing something, state your goal in terms of what you want to do instead.

2. Set a Deadline

Suppose you were learning archery but didn't have a target, so you just practiced by shooting in the air. How successful would you be in becoming skilled in archery? Chances are your progress would be slow. You need a target to shoot for. A deadline provides such a target. It gives you something to aim at.

3. Be Specific

Suppose you have a target, but you can't see where your arrow hits. Again, your shooting skill would develop very slowly. You need to see where the last shot went so that you can adjust your next shot. This feedback helps you *measure* your progress towards the goal. Measurability helps determine whether or not you have achieved your goal. The more specific your goal, the easier it is to measure your progress. Your goal statement should answer the following questions:

> ➢ Who?
> ➢ Will do what?
> ➢ When?
> ➢ Where?
> ➢ To what extent?
>   Under what conditions? To what degree?
>   How much? How long? How hard? etc.

Notice the emphasis on *doing*. What will the accomplished goal look like? What will you be doing? (Feeling? Saying? Having? Thinking?)

Examples of Poorly Written and Well Written Goals

Setting Better Goals

Remember that to be effective, goals should be positive, carry a deadline and be specific. Following are some examples of poorly written and improved goals.

> ➤ **Poor:** I will stop fighting with people in my department.

This goal statement violates all of the guidelines. It's negative, stating only what you want to stop doing. There is no deadline. And there is nothing to count: Measuring "not fighting" is difficult.

> ➤ **Poor:** I will improve my relationships at work.

This goal is stated positively. However, it violates the other two guidelines. What does an improved relationship look like? How will you recognize it? What you will be *doing* and which co-workers will be *doing* what when the relationship is "improved" are not specified. Finally, there is no deadline.

> ➤ **Better:** By the beginning of the year, I will socialize after hours with Ralph at least once a month.

There is a deadline and the goal statement is very specific. It will be easier to achieve this goal than the first two because you know what to do and when you have done it. An "improved relationship" has been defined in terms of what you will be doing: "socializing after hours." It states which co-worker is the target, and specifying the frequency and conditions of the socializing makes measurement possible.

Let's try another one.

> ➤ **Poor:** I will improve my time management by September 1st.

The goal statement is positive and there is a deadline. But it is still poorly stated because we don't know the *doing* of time management. What you want to do is vague, which makes it hard to know where to start and difficult to determine if and when the goal has been achieved.

"Time management" can be made more specific if you ask yourself: "What will I be *doing* when I've improved my time management?" Here are some examples:

> ➤ **Better:** By January 1 I will be able to satisfactorily complete all of my assignments and still have at least one hour per day available for discretionary work projects.

> ➤ **Better:** By Christmas I will be devoting at least two weekends a month to recreational activities.

The goal setting worksheet on the facing page may help.

Goal Setting Worksheet

What I want to accomplish during the next month:

1. _____

2. _____

3. _____

Select one of the desired accomplishments and write a **one month** goal statement.

MY ONE MONTH GOAL: _____

_____

Compare your goal statement to the goal-setting guidelines. Have you met all of them? Is it positive? Is there a deadline? Is it specific enough to measure? How can you improve your goal statement? Write your better goal statement here:

MY IMPROVED ONE MONTH GOAL: _____

_____

_____

What I want to accomplish during the next year:

1. _____

2. _____

3. _____

Now select one of the desired accomplishments and write a **one year** goal statement.

MY ONE YEAR GOAL: _____

_____

_____

Compare your goal statement to the goal-setting guidelines. Have you meet all of them? Is it positive? Is there a deadline? Is it specific enough to measure? How can you improve your goal statement? Write your better goal statement here:

MY IMPROVED ONE YEAR GOAL: _____

_____

_____

ACCOMPLISHING YOUR GOALS THROUGH SMALL STEPS

Inertia is defined as:

"a body at rest will tend to stay at rest and a body in motion will tend to stay in motion."

Imagine your car has a dead battery and you must push it to get it started. The greatest effort to get the car moving is the first push. This is when you break the inertia, and move the car from rest to motion.

The hardest part in accomplishing a goal is getting started. Before you begin working on your goal you are a body at rest. You must break the inertia and get your body into motion. Once you are in motion, it is easier to keep moving.

The secret to getting started: *take small steps.*

**Take
Small Steps**

Setting Objectives

Objectives are tools for making the steps needed to achieve your goal. An objective is a precise statement of what you plan to do during each step. Objectives can be thought of as mini-goals.

1. Break your goal into a series of smaller steps necessary to accomplish it.
2. Arrange the steps in a logical sequence.
3. Follow the Goal-Setting Guidelines described on page 21. When stating your first objective: Be specific. Be positive. Set a deadline.

1. Set Yourself Up to Win

Your small step should be only as big as what you *know* you can achieve with relative ease. If it is something difficult because it's distasteful or involves an entrenched habit, then shorten the time frame of the objective. For example, suppose you want to stop smoking. If, for your first objective, you demand that you will chew gum every time you feel like smoking for a month, you are likely to fail. Chances for success are better if you make the first objective for one day. When you meet that objective, set another one for a slightly longer period of time. Set objectives that you *know* you can meet. Set yourself up to succeed. The objective helps you get started and creates momentum. Once you've broken the inertia of a bad habit you have also started to develop a winner's attitude, which will also help you to succeed.

2. Stretch

Although objectives should be small steps, they should be big enough to make you stretch. Think of yoga as an example. When doing yoga you position your body in a particular posture and then slowly *s t r e t c h* the muscles you are exercising. Similarly, the series of small step objectives should slowly stretch your abilities. Don't worry about steps being too small. No step is too small as long as there is some stretch and some movement. Remember the inertia principle: A body in motion will tend to stay in motion. Use small steps to keep yourself in motion toward your goal.

3. Make Getting There Fun

People often equate self-management or self-discipline with austerity—the withholding of pleasures, or punishment. Such an approach is a mistake and will undermine your success. Grease the skids of change with fun. Enjoyment of a task lessens the toil of doing it. Consider physical exercising. Doing jumping jacks and running in place isn't much fun. By comparison, playing tennis with a friend is fun. And it provides a good workout. With this in mind, think of ways you can build fun into the process of achieving your goals.

One Month Objectives Worksheet

MY ONE MONTH GOAL (from page 23)

_____

_____

_____

_____

SMALL STEPS: First list, then sequence with 1 being the first step, 2 being the second, etc.

Sequence

____   _____

____   _____

____   _____

____   _____

____   _____

OBJECTIVE FOR FIRST STEP: Be Specific

What I will do: _____

Where — In what situation: _____

How much — To what degree: _____

By when: _____

One Year Objectives Worksheet

MY ONE YEAR GOAL (from page 23)

_____

_____

_____

SMALL STEPS: First list, then sequence with 1 being the first step, 2 being the second, etc.

Sequence

___ _____

___ _____

___ _____

___ _____

___ _____

OBJECTIVE FOR FIRST STEP: Be Specific

What I will do: _____

Where — In what situation: _____

How much — To what degree: _____

By when: _____

Rewards for Accomplishment

Giving yourself acknowledgment for what you've done well provides the motivational "wins" necessary to climb the small steps. Poor self-managers tend to do just the opposite. They focus on their failures and criticize what they did wrong. Self-criticism tends to set up a vicious cycle of "working to avoid," in which work is done to avoid guilt and anxious feelings. Self-acknowledgment, on the other hand, promotes "working for." It stimulates much better feelings.

Acknowledgment can be expressed in a variety of ways, such as by giving yourself things you want, by allowing yourself to do things you enjoy, or by giving yourself praise for things you have done well.

My Want List

Make a list of things you want. Include activities and social encounters you enjoy and things you want to continue doing. Give yourself items from your Want List as rewards and acknowledgment for meeting your small step objectives. These are pleasures you have earned!

Things I Want

_____

_____

_____

_____

_____

_____

_____

_____

_____

_____

_____

_____

My Want List (continued)

Activities I Like

_____

_____

_____

_____

_____

_____

_____

_____

_____

_____

_____

_____

_____

_____

The Self-Contract

Using a New Year's resolution can sabotage your good intentions. In this all-or-nothing approach you resolve to *never* again do whatever it is that you want to stop doing or to *always* do something you want to do. One transgression and you have failed. "Always" and "never" are impossible standards to meet.

On the other hand, the self-contract is a powerful tool for climbing the small steps to success. A self-contract is a written agreement that you make with yourself specifying the small step objective you intend to carry out and the "win" you will give yourself for doing it. A self-contract, like all contracts, has a term that states how long the agreement will last. Self-contract terms can be for a few minutes or for weeks, months or years.

Write a contract for *only as much change as you know you can accomplish.* Be sure that the time frame is short enough so that you know you can stick to your resolve. This is important. When the contract is fulfilled, give yourself a "win," and then move to the next step. Increase the amount, intensity, or quality of your performance, or the term of the contract. Successfully completed contracts are "wins" that fuel motivation.

The contract is a tool to get into motion and keep in motion. It is a way of teaching yourself to "work for" and to develop enthusiasm for work. Use the self-contract (or a copy of it) that is shown on the facing page.

 **SUMMARY OF SELF-MANAGEMENT
THE FIRST PATH TO PERSONAL POWER**

Effective self-mangement skills increase personal power and help prevent job burnout. When you can accomplish what you set out to do, you feel strong and in control of your job and your life. Self-management is the first path because you need it to follow the other seven paths to personal power.

Begin by setting goals. Be specific in stating what you will do, when, where and to what degree. Be positive and set a deadline. Then break your inertia by using small steps to get moving and to keep moving. Steps should be just large enough to make you stretch just a little bit. Set yourself up to win and make getting there fun. Remember your motivation must be fueled by "wins." Make a Want List and start giving yourself "wins" for meeting your small step objectives. Build your commitment by making a contract with yourself for each step. This is the way to become a Can-Do person.

Self-Contract

I will _____

_____

_____

_____

(Small Step)

When I complete this I will _____

_____

_____

_____

(Item from Want List)

_____

(Contract Term)

_____   _____

(Date)   *(Signature)*

STRESS MANAGEMENT

Second Path to Personal Power

Stress is the fever of burnout.

If you had pneumonia it would be essential to keep the accompanying fever down to avoid brain damage. But bringing down a fever will not cure pneumonia. The same is true with the stress that accompanies burnout. You must bring the stress down to preserve health, but reducing stress will not eliminate the underlying cause of burnout, which is a feeling of powerlessness.

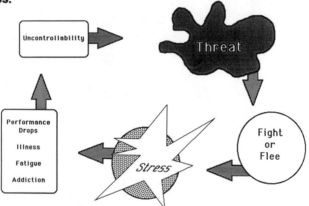

How Burnout Is Stressful

1. Loss of Control = Threat

One of the most serious threats we can encounter is uncontrollability. All animals, especially human beings, are concerned about controlling their respective worlds. Striving to control the world around us is a survival drive. When we feel a loss of control, we feel threatened, and this triggers the "fight-flight" response.

2. Fight-Flight

When confronted with threat, a body mobilizes to either fight the threat or flee from it. Muscles tense, blood rushes, breathing quickens. But when you neither fight nor flee, but remain in the powerless situation, the result is chronic stress.

3. Chronic Stress

It is this unrelenting chronic stress that causes many of the symptoms of burnout, such as exhaustion, health problems, irritability, intellectual impairment, and emotional outbursts. This is why stress must be treated.

Objective of Stress Management

The objective of stress management is to keep stress or tension levels within the optimal range for performance, health and well-being.

When levels of tension or stress are low, performance tends to be low as well. There is too little stimulation to keep attention on what is at hand. This is called boredom, understimulation, or depression.

At high levels of stress performance is also low, because stress impairs physical and intellectual functioning. In this state it feels as if you are simply spinning your wheels. High stress interferes with creative performance and may be manifested by hyperactivity, forgetfulness, frequent mistakes, lack of concentration, or irritability.

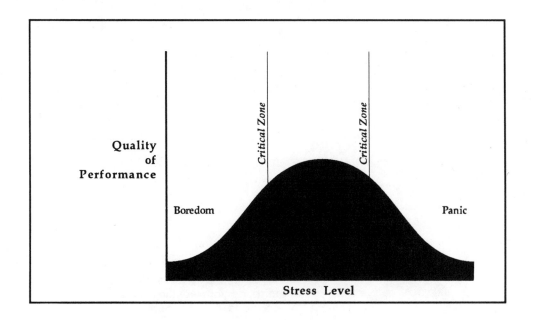

Controlling Stress

The first step to controlling stress is to identify situations that stress you and gather information on how you respond to them. Then you can see your response habits and develop a plan for change.

Create a Personal Stress Log

Each time you feel angry, upset, pressured, anxious, excited, worried or frustrated, stop and look at yourself and the situation. Create a stress log similar to the one shown below and note the following dates:

1. When did the event occur? What day and time?
2. What was the situation? Who was there? Where did it happen?
3. Rate your distress level, using a scale from 1 to 10, with 1 being "very little distressed" and 10 being "extremely upset."
4. How did you respond? What were your thoughts? How did you feel? What did you do?

When	Situation	Distress Level	Response: Thoughts, Feelings, Actions

When bored or depressed:

Increase your tension level. Look for problems to solve. Listen to upbeat music, take a cold shower, exercise, do your work in a peopled area such as the cafeteria, or eat hot spicy foods. These stimulating activities will increase tension level and help you move into the optimal range for performing.

When overstimulated:

Reduce tension level. Meditate, breath deeply, systematically relax your muscles, or imagine a relaxing scene. Listen to slow melodic music, take a warm bath, lie on a soft bed, watch fish swim in an aquarium, eat bland foods, or drink warm milk or herbal teas. If possible, consider giving yourself the day off.

CONTROL YOUR STRESS

Discover Your Personal Stress Patterns

Collect data on your stress responses for several days. Then review your Personal Stress Log (page 34), looking for patterns. What generalizations can you make about the times and situations that were distressing? Are deadlines a frequent cause for panic? Is there a particular person or type of event that appears several times in your Personal Stress Log? What responses do you use over and over? Do you eat when you feel anxious? Do you avoid certain situations?

Discover stress patterns by analyzing what the situations have in common. From this analysis, you can begin making a plan for managing stress. Are there situations you can avoid? Perhaps you can foresee stressors and prepare for the encounter? How might you respond more effectively?

Stress Patterns Analysis

Types of Patterns	My Usual Response	Possible Plan of Action
People		
_____	_____	_____
_____	_____	_____
_____	_____	_____
Places		
_____	_____	_____
_____	_____	_____
_____	_____	_____
Events		
_____	_____	_____
_____	_____	_____
_____	_____	_____
Time		
_____	_____	_____
_____	_____	_____
_____	_____	_____
Other: Specify		
_____	_____	_____

Stress Reduction Techniques

These are several ways for a person to reduce his or her level of stress. These will be discussed in the next few pages. They include learning how to breathe, recognizing tension, exercises to systematically relax muscles, and using your imagination.

Breathing Correctly

It seems crazy to explain the correct way to breathe because we tend to think it is something we do naturally. Yet, many people breathe shallowly and too much air remains in their lungs.

Slow deep breathing automatically relaxes: Even a few minutes of deep breathing will produce noticeable changes in tension level. Deep breathing can be used any time and any place. Several deep breaths just before a difficult situation is calming and increases feelings of control.

How to breathe: During inhalation the diaphragm contracts and descends. This increases lung capacity. During exhalation the diaphragm relaxes and moves upward, forcing air out. In other words, when you breathe in your abdomen should go out; when you breathe out the abdomen should go in.

Check your breathing: Place your hand on your abdomen and notice what happens when you breathe. Does your hand go out when you inhale and in when you exhale? Hold your hand on your abdomen the first couple of times you do this exercise to make sure you are breathing correctly. As you gain skill and lung capacity, slowly increase the inhale and exhale periods to six seconds, then to eight seconds.

> *Exercise:*

Step 1: Inhale slowly and deeply for four seconds, while counting 1-and-2-and-3-and-4. Notice the full feeling in your lungs.

Step 2: Exhale slowly for four seconds, while counting 1-and-2-and-3-and-4. Try to push out even more air.

Step 3: Repeat steps 1 and 2 while focusing all your attention on breathing and counting until you are able to increase your inhale and exhale periods to eight seconds.

Identifying Tension

Learning to relax in difficult situations increases personal power. You can keep tension within the optimal range during crisis and have all your resources to draw upon. You can be confident that you can stay cool while allowing your body to rest and repair as you prepare for optimal functioning.

Identifying tension level from moment to moment is the first step. "Oh, I know how tense I am," you may say. "I know when I'm uptight!" This is not always the case. In fact, most people do *not* accurately read their tension levels and are *not* aware of how inaccurate they can be. When you first become tense, it feels uncomfortable. But the discomfort fades rapidly, making it easy to misread tension level and miss a vital warning signal. It's like driving your car with a burned out oil level indicator bulb. You know how serious that can be!

> *Try this experiment:*

Procedure	Make a *very tight* fist with your left hand and continue holding it tight for 60 seconds.
Observe	Like a scientist, objectively study what you feel, where you feel it, and how intensely you feel it.
Procedure	After 60 seconds, make a *very tight* fist with your right hand while continuing to hold your left fist tight.
Observe	What are you experiencing in your right fist? How does this compare to what you feel in your left fist?

How to Sense Tension

With the following technique you can train yourself to sense tension in a short time. Start by discriminating between the sensations of tension and those of relaxation. Repeat the experiment several times until you become familiar with the sensations of tension and relaxation in the muscles in your hand.

> *Try this experiment:*

Procedure	*Lightly* tense your left fist. The degree of tension should be *just enough* to notice.
Observe	Like a scientist, objectively study what you feel in your fist. For seven to ten seconds *watch* exactly where and how the sensation of tension is for you.
Procedure	Create contrast by *quickly* opening your fist to release the tension and consciously relaxing the muscles in your hand.
Observe	Watch what you experience in your left hand. In a detached manner, compare how your hand feels when relaxed with how it felt when tense. Use this as a point of reference.

Systematically Relaxing Muscles

It takes about 25 minutes to systematically relax the muscles in your body. Here's how:

Procedure: Starting with your head and face and slowly moving down your body, tense and relax your muscles in the same way that you did with your fist (see page 37). Hold the tension for seven to ten seconds, except for the feet , which you should hold for only three to four seconds to avoid cramping. Study and compare the sensations of tension and relaxation in each muscle.

Breathing: Deep breathing helps to relax you. Breathe in during the tensing phase and out (see page 36) during the relaxation phase. Breathe deeply in and out before moving to the next muscle.

Talk to yourself: Just before you release the tension and exhale, tell yourself to "Relax." Eventually, you will learn to release tension in a particular muscle group by focusing your attention on it and telling yourself to relax. This is the Relax Command.

Tense ⇨ Observe
Relax ⇨ Observe

Compare

Tension vs. Relaxation

As you explore the various facets of personal power, you will see that the essential ingredient is self-observation. To know what stresses you, how you respond, how you think and how you feel requires your observation. Try the relaxation exercise on the facing page.

Relaxation Exercise

Instructions: With eyes closed, tense and relax each muscle, one at a time. Study the sensation of tension in the muscle. Think, "Relax," and then release the tension from the muscle, relaxing it as much as you can. Study the sensation of relaxation. Compare the sensations of relaxation and tension.

Face and Throat

Face: Squint eyes, wrinkle nose and try to pull your whole face into a point at the center.

Forehead: Knit or raise eyebrows.

Cheeks: While clenching the teeth, pull the corners of your mouth to your ears.

Nose and upper lip: With mouth slightly open, slowly bring upper lip down to lower lip.

Mouth: Bring lips together into a tight point then press mouth into teeth. Blow out gently to relax.

Mouth: Press the right corner of your mouth into your teeth and push the corner slowly toward the center of your mouth. Repeat for the left corner.

Lips and tongue: With teeth slightly apart, press lips together and push tongue into top of mouth.

Chin: With arms crossed over chest, stick out your chin and turn it slowly as far as it will go to the left. Repeat for right side.

Neck: Push your chin into your chest at the same time as pushing your head backwards into the back of your chair to create a counter-force.

Arms and Hands

Hand and forearm: Make a fist.

Biceps: Bend the arm at the elbow and make a "he-man" muscle.

Upper Body

Shoulders: Attempt to touch your ears with your shoulders.

Upper back: Push shoulder blades together and stick out chest.

Chest: Take a deep breath and hold it for several seconds.

Stomach: Pull stomach into spine or push it out.

Lower Body

Buttocks: Tighten buttocks and push into chair.

Thighs: Straighten leg and tighten thigh muscles.

Calves: Point toes towards your head.

Toes: Curl toes.

Do this exercise in a quiet, private place and notice when you finish how good it feels to be totally relaxed.

Relaxation Training Plan

Distressing Situations

Review your Personal Stress Log (page 34) and list the distressing situations in order, from the *least* distressing to the *most* distressing. Use the distress level ratings you made at the time that you observed yourself in the situations.

Distress Rating
(List least to most)

Distressing Situations

_____   _____

_____   _____

_____   _____

_____   _____

_____   _____

Self-Contract

Beginning with the least distressing situation, develop a plan of action for handling the situation. You might use deep breathing when you are in the situation. Or you might work on relaxing the muscles directly while thinking, "Relax." Then write a self-contract for practicing relaxing while in that situation. When you can handle the mildest situation and remain relaxed, move to the next situation on the list.

When _____

_____
(Least Distressing Situation)

I will _____

_____
(Plan for Relaxing)

When I have done this I will _____

_____
(Item from Want List)

_____   _____
(Date)   *(Signature)*

Practice Relaxing

A Quiet Spot

In the beginning it's a good idea to practice in a quiet spot that you already find relaxing. You might try a lawn chair in your backyard, or a comfortable sofa. Your bed is an old stand-by. But don't be surprised if you fall asleep!

My Quiet Spot for Relaxation Practice: _____

_____

At Work

After practicing in a quiet spot for about two weeks, slowly transfer the practice to your daily routine. The key here is *slowly*.

Relax your muscles: Instead of a coffee break, you might close your office door, turn off the lights, and spend five minutes tensing and relaxing muscles. Or you might practice during other times when you are waiting for the elevator, waiting on hold on the telephone, or waiting for a meeting to start.

Tell yourself to "Relax": Use the Relax Command. Take a deep breath and tell yourself to relax. Begin in mild tension-producing situations, such as riding the bus home from work. This is an ideal way to unwind for the evening. Or try it before making that phone call that you have been putting off.

Imagine a Pleasant Scene

Tension can be lowered quite rapidly by taking a few deep breaths and imagining a *pleasant scene*. A pleasant scene can be anything positive: a real situation, such as lying in a hammock in your backyard, or a pretend scene, such as riding on a billowy white cloud. There need be no limits. The only requirement is that imagining it relaxes you.

Your Pleasant Scene is a special place you can visit at any time and in any situation to relax and refuel. Just a three-to-four-minute visit will have a rejuvenating effect.

Visit your Pleasant Scene using the exercise on the next page just before a difficult situation, to take a break from demanding work, or to prepare for a change in activity.

VISIT YOUR PLEASANT SCENE ⟹

Write a Pleasant Scene

Write a description of a Pleasant Scene that you find relaxing. Add as much detail as you can. The more the scene stimulates your senses, the more powerful it will be in relaxing you.

Where I will be: _____

What I will see: _____

What I will hear: _____

What I will feel: _____

What I will smell: _____

Practice

Wiggle yourself into a comfortable spot; loosen your belt and shoes. With your eyes closed, breathe deeply to relax yourself. Imagine yourself *in* Your Pleasant Scene. Imagine all the detail you wrote on the paper. Bring it to life, making it as vivid as possible. Think about the details. Imagine with all your senses. Your pleasant scene may come more strongly through some of the senses than others. Don't worry about this. With practice your ability to imagine will improve. Don't look at yourself as a character on a TV screen. Put yourself *into* the situation. Imagine yourself *inside* your body during the scene. Notice new sights, smells, sounds, sensations, and tastes that you didn't write on the paper. After returning from your pleasant scene, add these new discoveries to the description of your scene.

Additions to My Pleasant Scene:

Where I was: _____

_____

What I saw: _____

_____

What I heard: _____

_____

What I felt: _____

_____

What I smelled: _____

_____

SUMMARY OF STRESS MANAGEMENT
THE SECOND PATH TO PERSONAL POWER

When you know that you can handle stressful situations, you feel more powerful. Not only will you protect your health, but you are likely to perform better and get more "wins." The increased "wins" and feelings of control help to buffer you against burnout situations at work.

Stress is the fever of burnout. And like a fever, you must bring the stress down in order to preserve your health. Keep a Personal Stress Log so that you can identify your stress response habits and develop a plan for change. Remember, you can relax by simply breathing slowly and deeply from the diaphragm. Greater relaxation can be achieved if you train yourself to relax your muscles. The key is to first lightly tense a muscle and study the sensation; then quickly release the tension and compare the feeling of relaxation to the feeling of tension. Breathe in while tensing and breathe out while relaxing. Use your self-managing skills to develop and carry out a relaxation training plan.

Imagining a Pleasant Scene is another powerful technique for relaxing. Your Pleasant Scene is a special place you can visit at any time and in any situation to relax and refuel. Don't wait until you're stressed; instead write your Pleasant Scene now. And practice using it to relax yourself. It's fun. It feels good. And it's healthy.

BUILDING SOCIAL SUPPORT

The Third Path to Personal Power

Social support acts as a buffer against stress and burnout. You can tolerate a greater degree of stress when you have caring and supportive relationships. In fact, research shows that people with close emotional and social ties are physically and mentally healthier and live longer!

Close friends and good relationships with co-workers and family reaffirm your competence and self-worth. They can help you to get things done and provide you with valuable information. They can help you handle difficult situations. They can listen to your problems and give feedback. They can help you learn new skills. They can encourage you to tackle challenges and accomplish goals.

Hints for Building Social Relationships

Invite others: Don't just wait to be invited. Start inviting others to do things with you. Ask co-workers to join you for lunch. Look through the paper for interesting events and ask a friend to accompany you. People love to be invited out.

Show interest in others: The most powerful resource you have for building social relationships is your attention. When you pay attention to others, they feel good about themselves and about you. Showing interest is easy. All you have to do is ask questions. Find out how others feel about community issues. Ask about hobbies. Be curious about what others want to accomplish.

Make others winners: It's easy to make others winners. All you have to do is notice what a person is doing well and comment on it. It only takes a minute. Try it.

Be helpful: When you help others accomplish their goals, they are inclined to want to help you, too. Helping doesn't take a lot of effort. Sometimes it is as easy as sharing information. Or you might introduce people to each other. Get outside of yourself and think about what you could do to help someone else. Even if nothing else comes of it, helping feels good.

Ask for advice: When you ask others for advice, they are flattered. They feel important. And they become committed to you. They want to see you succeed.

Make a Plan for Building Social Support

Relationships don't develop in a vacuum. You must create them. Think of specific things you can do today to start building your relationships.

What I can do to build my relationships with family and friends:

1. With _____
   I can _____
2. With _____
   I can _____
3. With _____
   I can _____
4. With _____
   I can _____
5. With _____
   I can _____

What I can do to build my relationships with co-workers:

1. With _____
   I can _____
2. With _____
   I can _____
3. With _____
   I can _____
4. With _____
   I can _____
5. With _____
   I can _____

What I can do to become involved in professional or social associations:

1. I can _____
2. I can _____
3. I can _____

Build a Network of Allies

The modern workplace is a social environment. Succeeding on the job requires more than just accomplishing tasks. It also means building productive relationships.

You can improve your effectiveness by taking time to build a network of allies. Allies can give you needed information, connect you with the right person, and open doors to valuable resources.

Effective people know how to find things out and how to get things done. The most effective people have allies throughout the organization. They cultivate friendly relationships in every division and help others. In turn, they can count on allies to help them.

Self-Contract for Building Social Support

Start building your social support system today. Don't put it off. Review the list of possible things you can do and decide upon one specific action to build your relationship with a friend, family member, or co-worker or in your professional organization. Then make a commitment with yourself to take action, NOW!

Use the self-contract. Write down exactly what you are going to do. When you will do it. And remember to give yourself a "win" for following through. You deserve all the "wins" you can get.

My Self-Contract for Building Relationships

By _____
(Deadline)

I will _____
_____
(Small Step)

When I complete this I will _____
_____
(Item from Want List)

_____   _____
(Date)   *(Signature)*

☞ ## SUMMARY OF BUILDING SOCIAL SUPPORT
THE THIRD PATH TO PERSONAL POWER

Social support acts as a buffer against the effects of stress. Allies on the job can help you get your job done. Consequently, when you have a strong social support system you feel potent, able to perform well and able to handle the inevitable problems. This helps prevent job burnout.

Make a plan for building social support and developing allies. And then act. Show interest in others and invite co-workers to events. Be helpful and make others winners by noticing their accomplishments. Stop right now and think of what you can do tomorrow at work to build social support. Make a commitment with yourself to do it by writing a self-contract.

SKILL BUILDING

The Fourth Path to Personal Power

> **You can't predict what skills the future will demand. Job security depends upon knowing how to acquire needed skills.**

Each job skill or ability enlarges your horizons and personal power. You can do more and have more of what you want. Mastery, knowing how to *do* and doing it well, feels good. You like yourself more and get more recognition from others. With self-confidence, you approach difficult situations with an *I-Can-Do* attitude. It is a chance to exercise your "skill muscles."

By contrast, when you lack needed skills others may claim you represent the Peter Principle because you appear to have reached your "level of incompetence." Without necessary skills to perform, it is difficult to win. Energy is devoted to avoiding negative situations rather than pursuing positive ones. Eventually you feel incompetent, incapable, and helpless to change it.

The next few pages will provide some ideas and techniques which will allow you to begin building new skills which will help you beat job burnout in the future.

SKILL BUILDING CHECKLIST

Skill Building Checklist

Review your Personal Stress Log (page 34) and your Stress Patterns Analysis (page 35). For each situation and pattern, consider what actions you might have taken or what abilities you might have exercised to reduce the distress. Think of others who would have handled the situation more effectively—what skill he or she would have used. For each situation and/or pattern, check the skill identified.

Skill Checklist

Skill	Skill
_____ Assertiveness	_____ Mentoring
_____ Decision making	_____ Networking
_____ Listening	_____ Leading meetings
_____ Information gathering	_____ Managing time
_____ Team playing	_____ Goal setting
_____ Delegating	_____ Relaxing
_____ Giving support	_____ Self-starting
_____ Getting support	_____ Self-acknowledging
_____ Public speaking	_____ Writing
_____ Specific technical skills	_____ Planning
_____ Negotiating	_____ Mediating
_____ Supervising	_____ Giving feedback
_____ Using feedback	_____ Prioritizing
_____ Other _____	_____ Other _____
_____ Other _____	_____ Other _____
_____ Other _____	_____ Other _____

Analysis

Tally the number of checks for each skill. Circle the five skills with the most checks. These are the skills you need to learn.

Skill Building Strategies

Following are four strategies that will help you to build your skills. Check those you plan to begin using.

❏ **Ask for feedback and advice**

Co-workers and friends see you in ways you don't see yourself. They see you in a more detached way. Ask others what they think you might do to improve your effectiveness at work. Listen to what they say and take advantage of their experience and advice.

❏ **Find role models**

One of the most effective ways to learn is by watching others. Identify people who are skilled at what you wish to learn. If you can't find anyone on your job or in your personal life, join a club or association, take a course to find role models, or study characters in books and films.

❏ **Coach yourself**

The best teachers are coaches. Coaches use good management techniques. Coaches set reachable targets and praise progress. Coaches give feedback on areas needing improvement and set small step objectives for the next shot at the target. Coaches are encouraging and supportive. Be your own coach.

❏ **Find a practice lab**

Practice is essential in skill building. Identify situations in which you can practice, then actively place yourself in situations that will demand that you use the skill. Set yourself up to win. Begin with easy situations. Sometimes this can be done as a hobby or activity away from the workplace.

My Skill Building Plan

Here's another opportunity to use self-management. First, go back and review pages 20–31. Then, specify your skill building plan below.

The skill I want to learn or improve _____

My Skill Building Goal: (Be positive. Be specific. Set a deadline)

_____

_____

Small Steps _____

_____

My Self-Contract for Taking the First Skill-Building Step

By _____
    (Deadline)

I will _____

_____
              (Small Step)

When I accomplish this I will _____

_____
              (Item from Want List)

_____   _____
        (Date)   *(Signature)*

☛ **SUMMARY OF SKILL BUILDING
THE FOURTH PATH TO PERSONAL POWER**

The modern workplace is constantly changing. We can not predict the future or know what skills we will need. We must become life long learners. If you know how to identify the skills you need and how to arrange a situation for learning them, you will feel confident to face an unknown future. People who can't, will increasingly find themselves "faking it." Eventually, their performance will decline and their opportunities will evaporate. They will be ripe for job burnout.

Skill building is an excellent opportunity to put your self-managing skills to work. First, identify what skills you want to learn or improve. Then set a goal that specifies what you will do. Remember to be positive and set a deadline. Break your learning sequence into small steps that you can achieve easily, yet make you stretch just a little. Make sure that you give yourself lots of "wins" for progress. Finally, bolster your commitment by writing self-contracts for each step.

Skill building is rooted in practice. Actively put yourself into situations that will require you to use your new skill. Seek out people who have the skill you want to learn. Ask for their advice and copy the way they do it. Finally, be your own coach. Give yourself reasonable targets and praise your progress.

TAILORING THE JOB

The Fifth Path to Personal Power

Virtually every job has some leeway to tailor it to fit the person doing the work. Often routines of the job are shaped more by the last person doing it than by the actual task. Yet, people forget that jobs are malleable. Instead, they implement the job in the same style as the last person. When that style doesn't fit, it is like trying to squeeze the round peg into the square hole. A job that doesn't fit can be abrasive to your motivation. Don't try to turn yourself into a pretzel. Tailor the job to fit you instead. In the process you will increase your personal power because you will feel in command of your work and you will probably do a better job. Here's how:

You were hired to provide a solution

You were not hired to do a job, but to solve a problem. For example, a person is not hired to file papers, but to solve a paper organization problem. What is the major problem you were hired to solve?

It is my responsibility to solve the problem of _____

_____

_____

_____

_____

Rating Tasks and Setting Priorities

Prioritizing Activities

Identify Tasks and Activities: List your tasks and activities at work. If you have difficulty remembering them, just close your eyes and *see* yourself in your work space, doing what you do at work. Notice the various tasks and activities. Do you answer the phone? Complete forms? Meet with co-workers? List them below.

Rate Impact: Using a scale from 1 to 10, with 1 being "no impact" and 10 being "great impact," rate the impact that each activity has upon the quality of the solution you were hired to provide.

Assign Priorities: Use the impact ratings to assign priorities to each task or activity. Assign an "A" priority for tasks with ratings over 7; "B" priority for ratings from 4 to 6; and "C" priority for ratings below 3.

Schedule: Use your priority rating system to schedule your day. Start with "A" tasks and activities. Try scheduling them directly on your calendar. Leave "C" priorities until last and, whenever possible, delegate them. What would happen if you didn't do the "C" activity at all? If the consequences are minimal, you might consider dropping the activity from your workload.

Task/Activity	Rate the		
	Impact	Priority	Enjoyment

Task Management

You have considerable discretion over when you do each task and how much time you spend on it. Are you taking advantage of the flexibility you have or are you doing the job in the way that last person did it? You can get a lot more done, avoid procrastination, and gain more satisfaction if you manage your tasks instead of letting them manage you.

Here's what to do:

Rate enjoyment: Review the tasks and activities you listed on page 53 and rate how much you enjoy each, using a scale from 1 to 9, with 1 being "unpleasant," 5 being "neutral," and 9 being "very pleasurable." Write your enjoyment rating in the last column of the table called "Rating Tasks and Setting Priorities."

Identify tasks you enjoy more and those you enjoy less: Starting with the "A" priorities, write the tasks in the table below. Put all the tasks you rated 4 or below in the column called "What I like doing less." Put the tasks you rated as 5 or above in the column called "What I like doing more."

Manage your tasks: First do a little work on tasks you "like doing less," then reward yourself with a little work from the list of tasks you "like doing more." With this technique you can beat procrastination. You'll be more effective and feel better about yourself. This is task management.

Tasks I Like More and Tasks I Like Less

Break complex tasks into several small steps, then list in the appropriate column

What I like doing less What I tend to put off	What I like doing more What I tend to do right away

Expand Your Job

Jobs are elastic. They can be stretched. Jobs are alive. They can grow and evolve. You can make your job stretch and grow to fit you better.

The best way to expand your job is to identify unattached problems. These are problems that have not been assigned to any specific person. Take possession of unattached problems you feel you can solve and that interest you. In most cases, this strategy doesn't require asking permission. Clever career strategists obtain formal authorization after the fact. Depending upon how important the solution is to the company, you might be able to use formally bestowed responsibility to obtain an upgraded job title, add support staff or services, or possibly even get a raise.

Identifying Unattached Problems

Close your eyes and *see* yourself at work. Run a typical work day across your mental stage. Recall an unusual day, and run it through. Notice what you do and what others do. What problems can you identify? Which problems fall outside of anyone's responsibility? List them below. While on the job, keep alert for problems, both big and small, that arise and list them. Don't overlook the obvious or mundane.

Analyze

Can you solve it? Write "S" next to those that you could solve.

Does it interest you? Write "I" next to those that interest you.

These are the "SI" or "yes" problems. Each of these problems is a potential area for job expansion.

Unattached Problems	I Can Solve It	It Interests Me

Brainstorm Solutions for Unattached Problems

Choose a "SI" problem

Review your list of "SI" problems and select one that falls close to your existing responsibilities.

Brainstorm possible solutions

Review in your mind the unattached problem you have decided to solve. Just "see" it occurring and study it. Describe the problem:

_____

_____

_____

Now, with your eyes closed, imagine the problem situation "fixed." At this point don't worry about the feasibility of the solution. Just "see" the problem corrected. Describe the solution.

_____

_____

_____

Now, close your eyes and see the problem fixed in a different way. Describe the second solution.

_____

_____

_____

Close your eyes and see the solution fixed in yet a third way. Describe the third solution.

_____

_____

_____

Continue this brainstorming until you come up with a solution that you believe is feasible and that _you_ can implement.

Make a Plan and Act

Set a Goal for Solving a "SI" Problem

My Goal: (Be positive. Be specific. Set a deadline.) _____

_____

_____

Identify the Small Steps for Implementing Your Solution

_____

_____

_____

_____

_____

_____

Identify Allies

Whose help will you need to implement your solution? List:

_____

_____

_____

Who might stand in the way or work against your plan? List:

_____

_____

_____

What resources will you need to implement your solution? Which allies can help you access those resources? List:

Resource	Ally

Self-Contract

Determine an action objective for the first step

By _____
(Date)

I will _____

_____
(Small Step)

When I accomplish this I will _____

_____
(Item from Want List)

_____   _____
*(Date)**(Signature)*

 ## SUMMARY OF TAILORING THE JOB
THE FIFTH PATH TO PERSONAL POWER

If your job doesn't fit your work style you can feel frustrated and perform less well than you are capable of doing. Over time such an ill fitting job can erode your motivation and contribute to job burnout. On the other hand, if you tailor your job to your style of working you will feel a greater sense of control over your work and thereby reduce the possibility of burning out.

Begin by determining the problem you were hired to solve. Then identify your tasks and activities at work and rate the impact each has upon your providing a solution to the problem you were hired to solve. Use this rating to prioritize your work. Rate your enjoyment of the high priority activities. Manage your tasks by working first on activities you enjoy less, then reward yourself by doing work you enjoy more. Task management will help you to become more productive and to get more satisfaction.

Expand your job by identifying unattached problems that interest you and that you can solve. Then make a plan and act. Remember, use your self-managing tools: Goal setting, small step objectives, contracting, and self-reward.

CHANGING JOBS

The Sixth Path to Personal Power

Some people wait until the job is intolerable, then race blindly into a new job. Without careful analysis and planning, there is little guarantee that the new job will be better. Many times it is worse! When you take time to analyze what is bothersome about your job and to determine what would be an ideal job *before* acting, you are much more likely to get a job that is right for you. In other words, analyzing what you don't like and do like increases your personal power and helps prevent job burnout.

The first question to ask is: Is the problem with the *type* of work or the job *situation*? Your answer will help determine if you should change your job or your career.

Consider These Cases:

Case 1: A nurse enjoys helping patients to understand their medical treatment and to feel more confident about it. But she is constantly at odds with her supervisor who says she's too slow on her rounds.

Case 2: A nurse enjoys the patients with whom he can chat. But his ward is housing stroke victims, many of whom have difficulty speaking. While intellectually he feels compassionate, he often gets irritated with the patients' slowness. He has snapped at patients more than once. His supervisor has criticized his attitude.

Case 3: A nurse feels depressed because the patients are annoying with their constant demands. What little enjoyment there is comes when dealing with record keeping and administrative matters.

Discussion:

The nurse in Case 1 enjoys her work but is having trouble with her supervisor's style. Changing jobs without first trying to change her job situation would be a mistake. She might solve the problem by learning how to manage her boss.

The nurse in Case 2 enjoys nursing but not the patients assigned to him. Chances are he can learn to control his irritation, but it is unlikely that he will ever like nursing verbally impaired patients. He is a candidate for a job change.

The nurse in Case 3 does not enjoy nursing. She sees patients' problems as demands. She seems to enjoy working with paper more than people. She is a candidate for a career change.

What About the Job
Is Getting You Down?

Identify Bothersome Situations

Review your Job Burnout Potential Inventory (page 16). List each item you rated as a 6 or higher on the table below under "Bothersome Situations." Next, close your eyes and project yourself mentally into your typical work day at work. Review it in your mind and notice what situations tend to make you feel frustrated or helpless. List these bothersome situations. Now bring to mind a particularly distressing day and identify what about it was bothersome. List these situations. The more specific you are, the better.

Analyze Patterns

Categorize the bothersome aspects of each situation. Use the following categories:

Environment: i.e., noise, poor lighting, crowded, fast pace

Management: i.e., lack of rewards, vague directives, favoritism

Co-workers: i.e., conflicts, politicking, cliques, rejection

Type of work: i.e., writing reports, helping people, keypunching

Other: specify what

Category	Bothersome Situations in My Job

Your Ideal Job

Review your analysis of the bothersome job situations. Which categories predominated? Look closer at those items. What do they have in common? Close your eyes and review each situation on your mental stage. What pattern do you see? List the pattern below.

Create a Picture of Your Ideal Job

Make yourself comfortable and use the relaxation techniques described on pages 32–43. Let your tension go. With your eyes closed, project one of the patterns listed below on your mental screen. Observe the bothersome apsect. Now envision a work situation in which this pattern did not occur. What would happen instead? What specific ways would be the job be different? Note this under "Ideal Scenario." Repeat the exercise several times with each bothersome pattern.

Bothersome Pattern: _____

Ideal Scenario: _____

Bothersome Pattern: _____

Ideal Scenario: _____

Bothersome Pattern: _____

Ideal Scenario: _____

Bothersome Pattern: _____

Ideal Scenario: _____

Bothersome Pattern: _____

Ideal Scenario: _____

Bothersome Pattern: _____

Ideal Scenario: _____

Envisioning My Ideal Job

Review the factors that you have identified as ideal in a job (page 62).
Once again, relax and project yourself into your ideal job. Weave in as
many aspects of the ideal scenario as possible. What mundane activities
would there be? What is the supervision style of your boss? Do you have
a boss? What is the environment like? *See* your work space. What are
co-workers like? Do you socialize with them? Where? Doing what?
The more complete the picture of your ideal job, the better. Describe it
below. Picture yourself in your ideal job again. Notice what you missed,
then add these details to your vision.

My ideal job title _____

The environment is _____

_____

Management is _____

_____

My boss is _____

_____

Co-workers are _____

_____

The mundane parts of the job are _____

_____

The interesting parts of the job are _____

_____

Other aspects of my ideal job are

_____

_____

_____

_____

_____

Transforming Barriers into Challenges

Under "Barriers," list everything standing between where you are now and your ideal job. Under "Challenges," list what you must do to remove the barrier. Don't be "realistic." Just write down what it would take to get around the barrier. Notice what you are thinking when you do this exercise. If you hear yourself saying a lot of reasons why you "can't," then list "negative thinking" as one of the barriers. Overcoming negative thinking is one of the greatest challenges of all.

Barriers	Challenges

MAKE A PLAN AND ACT

Make a Plan and Act

You can move toward your ideal job! Using the self-management techniques we discussed earlier (pages 20-31) is the winning approach. Choose a challenge, make a plan of action and then work on it in small steps. Make sure that you give yourself "wins" for success. Each day you will be a little closer to your ideal job. Each day you will feel more in control of your work and your life. Each day you will be taking action to prevent job burnout.

Choose a Challenge

Review your list of Barriers and Challenges and select a Challenge to work on.

To meet my challenge I would have to _____

My Goal (Be positive. Be specific. Set a deadline.) _____

Small steps _____

Getting Started

By _____
    (Deadline)

I will _____
_____
    (Small Step)

When I accomplish this I will _____
_____
    (Item from Want List)

_____   _____
    (Date)   *(Signature)*

 SUMMARY OF CHANGING JOBS
THE SIXTH PATH TO PERSONAL POWER

Sometimes the best way to prevent job burnout is to get a new job. Don't act impulsively, however. It is very important to pinpoint exactly what about the job is dampening your motivation as well as what would refuel it. This invaluable information well help you to feel more confident in your job search, to increase the chances that you will get a job that fits you and to prevent burning out.

THINKING POWERFULLY

The Seventh Path to Personal Power

Do you carry your frustrations with you?

The Muddy Road: A Zen Story

Two monks were walking along a muddy road when they came upon a beautiful woman unable to cross the road without getting her silk shoes muddy. Without saying a word, the first monk picked up and carried the woman across the road, leaving her on the other side. Then the two monks continued walking without talking until the end of the day. When they reached their destination, the second monk said, "You know monks are to avoid women. Why did you pick up that woman this morning?" The first monk replied, "I left her on the side of the road. Are you still carrying her?"

You feel what you think!

Your mind is always filled with thoughts and images. The mental chatter is always there. And the thoughts and images in your mind determine your mood.

If you think powerless thoughts and envision yourself as losing, you will feel powerless: depressed, anxious, frustrated, angry. These feelings perpetuate job burnout.

If you think powerful thoughts and envision yourself as winning, you will feel powerful: hopeful, enthusiastic, confident, energized. These feelings help prevent job burnout.

You Feel What You Think

Notice how you feel: Survey your body and emotions. Using a scale from 1 to 10, with 1 being "very negative," and 10 being "very positive," rate how you feel right now.

My mood rating _____

Make your mind blank: A blank mind contains no thoughts, no images, no colors. Nothing at all. Keep your mind blank for 60 seconds.

What happened? Did thoughts intrude and images scurry by? It is impossible for most people to make their minds blank without intensive mental training. Your mind is constantly filled with thoughts and images.

Recall an unpleasant situation: For 60 seconds, project yourself back into that scene. Make it as vivid as possible. Notice how your body feels and how you respond. Rate your mood again, using the same 1 to 10 scale.

My mood rating _____

Physical sensations I experienced _____

What I experienced during the actual situation _____

Recall a pleasant situation: For 60 seconds, relive a time when you were feeling good and doing well, making it as vivid as possible. Notice how your body feels and how you respond. Rate your mood again, using the same 1 to 10 scale.

My mood rating _____

Physical sensations I experienced _____

What I experienced during the actual situation _____

What Happened?

Did your mood state drop after recalling the unpleasant situation? What happened to your body? Did you feel tension? Did your heart race? How did your body react in the actual situation? Was it similar? How did you feel after recalling the pleasant time?

Develop an I-CAN-DO Attitude

Attitude is a style of thinking.   People with No-Can-Do attitudes think negatively and feel powerless. They continually tell themselves that they "can't." People who think positively focus on what they can do. They have an I-Can-Do attitude. Consequently, they feel powerful. They feel optimistic. They rise to challenges. No-Can-Do thinking makes you feel bad. It can even damage your health. I-Can-Do thinking fuels motivation and helps prevent job burnout.

Rid yourself of negative thinking. Translate each helpless thought into a powerful one. Powerful thoughts make you feel potent and help you act to influence the situation for the better. Powerful thinking is looking at the glass as half full rather than as half empty.

Helpless Thought	Powerful Thought
How could I have been so stupid?	I made a mistake and I can learn from my mistakes.
I really blew it this time. I'm a fool!	Next time I can . . .
My boss is such a lousy supervisor. I never know what he expects.	It would be nice if my boss would be clear in his expectations. This is a chance to practice my assertive skills. I must learn how to express my concern without alienating him.
I might lose control and start yelling at them. I'd better take a valium.	I'll make a plan for what I can do to handle my temper. Next time I can . . .
She is so inconsiderate of me.	I'd like it if she'd call when she's late but she doesn't. Figuring out how to handle this is a challenge. Next time I can . . .

Exercise in Powerful Thinking

Change Your Helpless Thoughts to Powerful Ones

List your habitual negative thoughts. Include all the reasons you tell yourself for not doing what you want to do; faults, failures and disappointments that you think about; others' wrong doings that haunt you; guilts you worry about; dissatisfactions you dwell upon; unhappy memories you recall often; and any other negative thoughts you ruminate about. Then translate each helpless thought into a powerful one.

Helpless Thought	Powerful Thought

Thought Stopping: Taking the Bummer by the Horns

The Mind Is Like a Wild Elephant

The mind is like a wild elephant that you must master. In mastering a wild elephant you begin by chaining it. But when first chained it rears up on its hind legs, throws its trunk back and roars. It flaps its ears, slaps its tail, and runs. If you are a good elephant trainer you don't scold the elephant, but simply grab the chain and pull it back. The elephant will try to run away again and again. When this happens you must pull it back. Again and again the elephant will rebell and again and again you must pull it back. Eventually, the elephant will be tamed when it learns that you are its master. Then you will have great power because you can climb up on the elephant and ride it fast and far. And the elephant no longer will have to wear its chain because it learned who its master is.

Training Your Mind

Think the helpless thought: Close your eyes and begin thinking one of your helpless thoughts. Repeat it over and over in your mind in the way that you typically do. Notice how you feel as you do this.

Then Yell "Stop!": Inside your mind, not out loud, yell "Stop!" at the helpless thought.

Switch to a powerful thought: Immediately change to a powerful thought. If the helpless thought creeps back in, just yell "Stop!" again, and pull your attention back to the powerful thought. No matter how many times your mind runs to the helpless thought, pull it back to the powerful one, again and again. Notice how you feel while thinking the powerful thought. Repeat this practice several times with each of the helpless thoughts.

Watch your thoughts: Whenever you catch yourself thinking one of your helpless thoughts, yell "Stop!" and pull your mind back to a powerful one. Compliment yourself for your successes in training your mind.

Keep practicing: We never have our minds fully trained. Rather, we can get better and better with practice. At least once a day, tell yourself to think one of your powerful thoughts. Develop a habit of talking powerfully to yourself. Compliment yourself whenever you notice yourself thinking a powerful thought.

**SUMMARY OF THINKING POWERFULLY
THE SEVENTH PATH TO PERSONAL POWER**

Your mood is determined by the thoughts in your mind. Chronic helpless thinking is a major contributor to job burnout. When you think powerfully you feel more powerful and are better equipped to take appropriate action to correct distressing situations at work—and at home.

Begin by translating your habitual negative thoughts into powerful ones. When you catch yourself thinking a negative thought, yell "Stop!" to stop the negative thought. Then, immediately switch your thinking to the powerful thought. Training the mind is difficult. So remember to reward yourself generously for your successes.

DETACHED CONCERN

The Eighth Path to Personal Power

Helping professionals must demonstrate concern for clients to be effective. But there is a danger of over-involvement. What if the client doesn't improve? Salespeople are expected to sell. What if the economy is in a recession? Teachers want to teach. What if the students won't learn? What if you have a truely impossible job? What if the "wins" are too few and there is nothing you can do? What if your job is terrible but you can't change it and can't leave it?

> **Detached concern is a delicate balance of involvement and nonattachment.**

Good Sportsmanship

Play to win (be concerned), but don't insist upon winning (be detached). Athletes who *must* win inevitably fumble and lose. How you shoot the arrow is more important than hitting the target. Whether you are a chief executive or a newly hired clerk, a social worker or a paper pusher, immerse yourself in the moment, in the *doing,* and let go of the outcome, good or bad. Don't demand wins. Events will not always be to your liking and you will not always win. Let losing teach you how to shoot the arrow next time. But don't cling to losing, either. Like the monk walking along the muddy road, leave the negative situation on the side of the road.

The Mirror

The mirror teaches "acceptance" or nonevaluation. When you step before a mirror, it reflects you. It doesn't evaluate who you are or wonder if it should reflect you. It simply reflects. The mirror exhibits "concern" because it reflects you totally and not half-heartedly. It does the best it can. And the mirror teaches "detachment." When you step away from the mirror it stops reflecting you. It doesn't protest, it simply lets you go.

Mother Theresa

A reporter asked, "How can you stand it? You work with sick and dying children, and they die anyway." The Nobel prize winning nun replied, "We love them while they are here." Mother Theresa is concerned and loves the children, yet she is detached. If they die, she lets them go.

Be Here Now

A monk was walking through the jungle when he encountered a hungry tiger. So he ran until he came to a ravine with a vine hanging over the edge. He climbed down until he saw a hungry tiger below. Safe for the moment, he listened and heard the gnawing noise of mice chewing on the vine. The monk was doomed. So he looked about and saw a strawberry plant with one luscious berry growing from the side of the ravine. He popped it into his mouth, and just as the vine snapped, he said, "Ah, delicious!" Don't dwell on past bummers or worries about the future. Live fully in the present moment—whatever you are doing.

Be Yielding

Each day during the winter snow fell on two trees in a field. The firm limbs of the big oak tree supported the snow until the branches, no longer able to bear the weight, broke and fell. Next to the oak tree, a pine tree also accumulated snow. But its limbs were supple, not rigid. They bent to the ground and let the snow slide off, then returned to their original position. The pine tree survived the winter, but the oak did not. Like water flowing downstream, flow around the rocks in life. Be flexible. Don't be attached to a particular notion of the way things ought to be. Look for alternative and creative ways to reach your goals.

Shift Your Viewpoint

Philosopher Alan Watts once said, "Problems that remain persistently insolvable should always be suspected as questions asked in the wrong way." Do you trap yourself in damned-if-you-do, damned-if-you-don't situations by the way you look at things? Think about things in new ways. See problems as opportunities, and see hassles as teachers.

Laugh a Lot

When you catch yourself taking things too seriously, laugh. Think of the "cosmic chuckle" and of the absurdity of it all. Satirize your distress. Imagine yourself in a Charlie Chaplin script. As a discipline, practice finding humor in disaster. You'll save your sanity, your health and your perspective.

 SUMMARY OF DETACHED CONCERN
THE EIGHTH PATH TO PERSONAL POWER

If your job is distressing and you cannot change it or leave it, then strive for detached concern. Make your best effort and don't dwell upon whether you are winning or losing. Instead, roll with the punches, focus on the present, think of problems as opportunities, and make sure to laugh a lot.

REVIEW

1. Job burnout is an impairment of enthusiasm and motivation caused by feelings of powerlessness at work. It is a destructive process that affects the victim's health, relationships, and performance. Common burnout symptoms include frequent illness, feelings of fatigue, irritability, substance abuse, withdrawal, absenteeism and declining job performance.

2. Burnout can be prevented by adequate amounts of motivational nutrients:

   "Wins" for good work: Wins are essential to maintaining high levels of motivation. Wins include acknowledgment, feelings of satisfaction, rewards and other positive outcomes for doing good work.

   Feelings of control: To remain motivated you must feel that you can influence what happens to you by what you do.

3. Burnout is cured by developing "personal power":

   Personal power is a feeling of I-Can-Do, a feeling that you can act to increase the wins and reduce the losses you receive. Personal power is a feeling of potency, a feeling that you can influence others and change situations in desired ways.

4. There are many paths to personal power. The eight covered in this book are:

   ❖ **Self-management** is using techniques such as goal setting and self-acknowledgment to sustain motivation and do what you set out to do.

   ❖ **Stress management** is moderating your physical and emotional responses to stressors for maximum health and performance.

   ❖ **Building social support** increases your effectiveness on the job and buffers you from the effects of stress.

❖   **Skill building** helps you adapt to a changing workplace, increases your effectiveness, and promotes self-confidence.

❖   **Tailoring the job** to you makes working more enjoyable and maximizes your ability to perform at your peak.

❖   **Changing jobs** removes you from the burnout situation. However, finding the right job for you requires analysis of the burnout factors in your old job and insight into your workstyle and interests.

❖   **Powerful thinking** leads to an I-Can-Do attitude. The way you think influences how you feel. Negative thinking underlies anger and depression whereas powerful thinking promotes feelings of personal power.

❖   **Detached concern** helps you to deal with situations that offer few wins and that you cannot change.

5. Developing personal power in not a one-time endeavor. Rather, it is a lifelong process of learning how to handle difficult situations.

ABOUT THE AUTHOR

Beverly A. Potter, Ph.D., earned her doctorate in counseling psychology from Stanford University and her masters in vocational rehabilitation counseling from San Francisco State University. She is a member of the Staff Development programs at Stanford University and Stanford Medical School. Her workshops for professionals and managers are sponsored by University of California at Berkeley and San Francisco State University. Dr. Potter has conducted training for a wide range of corporations, governmental agencies and associations including Hewlett-Packard, TRW-CI, Tap Plastics, California State Bar Association, California State Disability Evaluation, Department of Energy, International Association of Personnel Women and The Design Management Institute. Her offices are located in Berkeley, California.

Other books by Beverly Potter

Beating Job Burnout: Transforming Work Pressure into Productivity, Ronin Publishing.

Maverick Career Strategies: The Way of the Ronin, AMACOM, a division of the American Management Associations.

Turning Around: Keys to Motivation and Productivity, AMACOM and Ronin Publishing.